A RED CHERRY ON A WHITE-TILED FLOOR

A Red Cherry on a White-tiled Floor

SELECTED POEMS

Maram al-Massri

Translated by Khaled Mattawa

 Copper Canyon Press
Port Townsend, Washington

Copyright 1997, 2000, 2004, 2007 by Maram al-Massri

Translation copyright 2004, 2007 by Khaled Mattawa

First published 2004 by Bloodaxe Books Ltd., Highgreen, Tarset, Northumberland NE48 1RP

Cover art: Lara Baladi, *The Banquet, Larabesque Aroussa Baladi,* 2002. Permanent pigment print on somerset paper, 60 × 80 cm.

Copper Canyon Press is in residence at Fort Worden State Park in Port Townsend, Washington, under the auspices of Centrum, a gathering place for artists and creative thinkers from around the world, students of all ages and backgrounds, and audiences seeking extraordinary cultural enrichment.

LIBRARY OF CONGRESS CATALOGING-IN-PUBLICATION DATA

al-Massri, Maram.
[Karazah hamra' 'alá balat abyad. English & Arabic]
A red cherry on a white-tiled floor: selected poems / Maram al-Massri; translated by Khaled Mattawa.
    p.   cm.
English and Arabic.
"First published 2004 by Bloodaxe Books Ltd."
ISBN 978-1-55659-264-5 (pbk.: alk. paper)
I. Mattawa, Khaled.   II. Title.
PJ7846.I817K3713   2007
892.716–dc22

                                        2007010735

9 8 7 6 5 4 3 2   FIRST PRINTING

COPPER CANYON PRESS
Post Office Box 271
Port Townsend, Washington 98368
www.coppercanyonpress.org

ACKNOWLEDGMENTS

This book presents a selection of poems from two book-length sequences. The first, *Karzatun Hamraa ala Balatin Abyad* (*A Red Cherry on a White-tiled Floor*), was published by Éditions de L'or du temps, Tunis, in 1997; the second, *Andhur Elaik* (*I Look to You*), was published by La Société d'Éditions et de Publication, Beirut, in 2000. Some of the translations have appeared in *Banipal* (U.K.), *Lyric Poetry Review* (U.S.), and *Rattapallax* (U.S.).

CONTENTS

A RED CHERRY ON A WHITE-TILED FLOOR

مـن

كــرزة حمــراء على بــلاط أبيــض

١٩٩٧

from

A Red Cherry on a White-tiled Floor

1997

١ أنا سارقة السَّكَاكِر،
أمام دكانك
دَبَّقْتُ أصابعي
ولـم انجح
بوضع واحدة في
فـمي .

٢ يا للغـبـاء
قلبي في كل مرة يسمع نقراً
يَـفْتَحْ .

٣ تُشعلني الرغبة
وتتألق عيناي
أحشر الأخلاق في أقرب دُرج،
أتقمص الشيطان،
وأعْصُب عيون ملائكتي
من أجل
قُـبـلـة .

4

1   I am the thief
    of sweetmeats
    displayed in your shop.
    My fingers became sticky
    but I failed
    to drop one
    into my mouth.

2   How foolish:
    Whenever my heart
    hears a knocking
    it opens its doors.

3   Desire inflames me
    and my eyes glimmer.
    I stuff morals
    in the nearest drawer,
    I turn into the Devil
    and blindfold my angels
    just
    for a kiss.

٥   أنتظر،
وماذا أنتظر؟
رجلاً يأتي محملاً بالزهور،
وبكلمات جميلة.
رجلاً
ينظر إليّ ويراني.
يحدثني ويسمعني.
رجلاً يبكي
لأجلي
فأشفق عليه
وأحبه.

٦   رأيت آثار
الأقدام
نقاطاً سوداء
ذاهبة آتية.
الثلج الأبيض
الذي قيل عنه
نقي،
فضح
العصافير والقطط
وأشباح أفكاري،
قبل أن تأتي الشمس الكسولة،
لتمحو
كل ذلك.

5   I wait,
but what do I wait for?
A man who brings me flowers
and sweet words,
a man
who looks at me and sees me.
He talks to me and listens to me.
A man who weeps
for me
and I pity him
and I love him.

6   I saw
foot traces,
black spots
coming and going.
The white snow,
they said
was pure,
betrayed
the sparrows and cats
and the ghosts of my thoughts
before the lazy sun rose
and erased them
all.

٧ طرقات على الباب.
من؟
أُورِي غُبار وحدتي
تحت سجّادتي،
أرتِّب ابتسامتي،
وأفتح.

٨ غريب ينظر إليّ،
غريب يحدثني.
لغريب أبتسم،
لغريب أتحدث.
غريب يسمعني،
أمام
أحزانه البيضاء النظيفة
أبكي
للوحدة التي تجمع
الغرباء.

7   Knocks on the door.
    Who?
    I sweep the dust of my loneliness
    under the rug.
    I arrange a smile
    and open.

8   A stranger looks at me,
    a stranger speaks to me.
    To a stranger I smile,
    to a stranger I speak.
    A stranger listens to me
    and at
    his clean white sorrows
    I weep
    to the loneliness that gathers
    strangers.

٩ يدخلون حياتنا
كالجداول الصغيرة،
فإذا بنا
نغرق بهم،
ولا نعود نعرف
من أعطانا
ماءً وملحاً،
ومن ترك
فينا تلك
المرارة.

١١ وحدها
لم أدْعُها،
تجيء لزيارتي.
تحوم حولي
أطرُدُها
فإذا بها
كذُبابة سوداء
كذُبابة سوداء بشعة
تطير هنا، تطن هناك
وتحط في قعر قلبي.
الكآبة
بقرة بلهاء،
تجترّ
الأخضر واليابس
من غبطتي.

9   They enter our lives
    like small streams
    and suddenly
    we drown in them
    and become unaware
    of who gave us
    water and salt
    and left in us
    that
    bitterness.

11   Alone—
    I never let her
    visit me.
    She hovers around me
    and I kick her out.
    Then she becomes
    like a black fly,
    an ugly black fly,
    zips here, buzzes there,
    and lands in the bottom of my heart.
    Melancholy,
    a crazed cow,
    devours
    the green and dry
    shoots of my ecstasy.

١٢ دقيقة على جانبي
الأيسر.
دقيقة على جانبي
الأيمن.
قليلا على ظهري،
برهةً على بطني.
أدور في الفراغ
بردٌ في أحلامي
بردٌ في سريري.
لصوص النوم غزوا ليلتي؛
واحدٌ منهم
أشفق عليّ
وترك لي الصباح
على الطاولة.

١٣ من أين يأتي هذا الغبار؟
من أين يأتي؟
تمر بكفك عليه لتمحوه
لكنه دائماً يعود
كالوجوه
كالأصوات.
تظنه يتوسد السطوح
وإذا به يملأ الأعماق.

من أين تأتي هذه الذكريات
من أين تأتي...

12   A minute on my left
side,
a minute on my right
side,
a little on my back,
a while on my stomach,
I spin in emptiness.
Cold in my bed.
Cold in my dreams.
The thieves of sleep
have raided my night.
One of them
pitied me
and left me the morning
shining on the table.

13   Where does this dust come from?
Where from?
You pass your palm over it to wipe it,
but it always returns
like the faces,
like the voices.
You think it only covers surfaces,
but you realize that it fills the depths.

Where do these memories come from?
Where do they come from?

١٤ النساءُ مثلي
لا يَعرفْن الكلامَ:
الكلمة تبقى في الحلق
كالشوكة،
يُفضّلنَ بلعها.
النساءُ مثلي
لا يعرفن سوى البُكاء،
البكاء المستعصي
فجأة
ينهمر
كشريان مقطوع.
النساء مثلي
تَتَلَقَّينَ الصفعات،
ولا يجرُؤن على ردِّها.
يرتجفن من الغضب
يكبحْنَه.
كأسد في قفص
النساءُ مثلي
يحلمن...
بالحريــة....

14   Women like me
      do not know how to speak.
      A word remains in their throats
      like a thorn
      they choose to swallow.
      Women like me
      know nothing except weeping,
      impossible weeping
      suddenly
      pouring
      like a severed artery.
      Women like me
      receive blows
      and do not dare return them.
      They shake with anger,
      they subdue it.
      Like lions in cages,
      women like me
      dream…
      of freedom…

١٦   إنها تفتح لي
أبوابها العريضة.
إنها تناديني
وتدفعني لأن أطلق
نفسي في
فضائها،
وكعُصْفور
أمام باب قفصه المفتوح
لا أجرؤ.

١٧   حيث الأحصنة
لا تستطيع الركض.
حيث لا يوجد
ثغرة
تسمح
لشعاع من الضوء أن يدخل.
حيث لا عشب
ينبتُ؛
أتشبث
بأقدام الكلمة.

١٩   أربطها
بين الفك والحنك
بقماشة بيضاء
أشدها وراء رقبتي

16 It opens
    its wide doors to me.
    It calls me
    and nudges me forward
    to release myself
    into its space,
    and like a sparrow
    at the gate of its open cage
    I do not dare.

17 Where horses
    cannot gallop,
    where there is no
    crack
    to allow
    a beam of light to pass,
    where no grass
    grows,
    I cling
    to the feet of the word.

19 I tie it
    between jaw and chin
    with white cloth.
    I drag it from the back of my neck

كالموتى
كالسجناء
لئلا
تَدْوي.

٢٠   قتلت أبي
تلك الليلة
أو ذاك النهار
لم اعد أدري،
هاربة بحقيبة واحدة
ملأتُها بأحلامٍ دونَ ذاكرة،
وبصورة لي
معـه
وأنا صغيرة
يحملني
على زنده.

دفنت أبي
في صَدَفَةٍ جميلة
في محيطٍ عميق،
لكنه وجدني
مختبئةً تحت السرير
أرتجف من الخوف
والوحدة.

18

like the dead,
like prisoners,
so it would not
resound.

20   I killed my father
that night
or the other day—
I don't remember.
I escaped with a suitcase
filled with dreams and amnesia
and a picture of me
with him
when I was a child
and when he carried me
on his forearm.

I buried my father
in a beautiful shell,
in a deep ocean,
but he found me
hiding under the bed
shaking with fear
and loneliness.

٢١ في كل مرة
أفتح حقيبتي
يخرج غبار.

٢٢ طلبتُ منه
حُلماً،
فوهبها حقيقة.
من يومها
وجدت نفسها
ثكلى.

٢٣ سأنتظر
أن ينام الأطفال،
لأتْرُك
جُثَّة خيبتي
تطفو
على السطح.

٢٤ غُط في نومِكَ،
ولا تُعِر انتباهاً
لسُهادي،
اتركني أحلُم قليلاً
بطرقات مشجرة

21   Each time
I open my bag
dust blows out of it.

22   She asked him
for a dream
and he offered her a reality.
Since then
she found herself
a bereaved mother.

23   I will wait
until the children sleep
then let
the corpse of my failure
float
to the ceiling.

24   Deepen your sleep
and pay no mind
to my insomnia.
Let me dream a little
of tree-lined roads

وسهولٍ شاسعة،
أنطلق فيها
بأحصنتي الشَبِقَة.
أنا المرأة التي عليها أن تكونَ
عاقلة
ورزينة،
في الصباح.

٢٦   اشترى
يوماً
دمية،
تبتسم إذا أمرها بالابتسام،
تغني وترقص
إذا ضغط زرها،
وتنام إذا مددها.
يا لغضبه؛
الدمية أحياناً
تبكي،
و احياناً تظل فاتحة عينيها
وهي مُمدَّة.

and wide meadows
that I ride through
on my wild horses.
I am the woman who has to be
reasonable
and poised
in the morning.

26   One day
he bought
a doll.
She smiled
when he ordered her to smile,
she sang and danced
when he pressed her button,
and slept
when he laid her down.
But oh his rage!
The doll
laid out in his bed
sometimes weeps
and stares with wide-open eyes.

٢٧   نظرتُ إليه
عبرَ خيطٍ من الضوء
آتٍ
من شباك رحمتي.
الجسدُ المتعب
الذي يتمدد قربي
جائعاً مثلي.
أشرت ليَدِي أن
تقترب،
فلم تطاوعني.
أمرتُها
فعاندتني.
أجبرتُها.
اقتربت مرتجفة من الألم
للَمْسِ
جَسد آخر.

٢٨   جسد المرأة
ينتفض على حافة السرير.

عطشٌ..
و نهرٌ ما يفيض.

عطشٌ..
ونبع ما يترقرق.

24

27 I looked at him
   through a thread of light
   beaming from
   the window of my mercy—
   the tired body
   spread beside me
   hungry like mine.
   I signaled to my hand
   to come closer
   and it refused,
   I commanded it
   and it disobeyed.
   I forced it,
   and it bent closer
   shivering with the pain
   of touching
   another body.

28 A woman's body
   trembles on the edge of the bed.

Thirst

        and somewhere a river floods.

Thirst

        and a stream trickles.

جسد المرأة يشيخ.
أصابع الضجر
لا تنعشه،
و الرعشة
لا تمنحه الضوء.

٢٩   أعطني
حباً
كفاف يومي،
ولا تثقل على قلبي الحزين
بمثقال ذرة.
خذني
ولا تضربني بوردة.
غضّ الطرف
عن أخطائي،
وابعث برسلٍ
قبل أن تطأ أرضي.

٣٠   ساعدْني يا زوجي الطيب
أن أغلق
هذه الكَوّة
التي انفتحت
في أعلى حائط
صدري.

A woman's body ages.
The fingers of boredom
do not refresh it
and the tremors
      give it no light.

29   Give me
    love
    for daily rations
    and don't burden my sad heart
    even with a single atom.
    Take me
    and don't strike me with a rose.
    Lower your gaze
    before my errors
    and send messengers
    before you tread my earth.

30   Help me,
    my kind husband,
    to close this porthole
    that has opened
    on the highest wall
    of my chest.

امنعني يا زوجي الحكيم
أن اعتلي
كَعْبَ أنوثتي،
فعند مفترق الطريق
شاب
ينتظرني.

٣١ امرأة تعود
برائحة رجل غريب
إلى دارها.
تغتسل،
تتعطّر.
تبقى فواحةً
رائحة الندم.

٣٣ لا شيء أكثر
كآبة
من رؤية
رجل وامرأة
والملل ثالثهما.
رجل وامرأة
قد خمدت أحلامهما،
ولم تعد هنالك أشياء بلا أهمية
يقولانها.

Stop me, my wise husband,
from climbing
the high-heels of my femininity,
for there at the crossroads
a young man
awaits me.

31   A wife returns
with the scent of a man
to her home.
She washes,
she puts on perfume,
but it remains pungent,
the smell of regret.

33   Nothing more
depressing
than seeing
a man and a woman,
boredom their third companion,
a man and a woman
whose dreams have gone out
and who no longer have
useless things
to tell each other.

٣٤   لأنه لم يعد بيننا
حساء دافئ نتناوله
حديث فاتر نكرره.

لأنه لم يعد بيننا
غير سرير
لا تنبت عليه إلا الطحالب
وليل لا يمحو
تعب النهار.

لأنه لم يعد بيننا
سوى أطفال
نجهز لهم
أوهامنا
على طبق.

لأنه أصبحنا
أكثر من الغرباء تهذيباً
وأقل من الأعداء إعجاباً

لأنه لم يعد بيننا
تلك الضحكات الشجية
تلك اللمسات الصافية
وطعم
الغار والعسل
على شفاهنا.

34 Because between us
     there is no warm soup to eat
     and lukewarm words to repeat...

     Because between us
     there is no longer anything
     except a bed
     where only mushrooms grow
     and night that does not erase
     the weariness of the day...

     Because between us
     there is nothing
     but children
     whom we serve
     our delusions
     on a plate...

     Because we have become
     more polite than strangers
     and less than enemies
     in our mutual admiration...

     Because between us
     there are no longer
     any unbridled laughs
     and innocent touches
     and the taste

لأنه لم يعد
بيننا.

٣٥ أنا أعتذر،
لأني من حيث
لم أنتبه
هبت نسائمي
على أغصانك،
فأوقعت
الزهرة الوحيدة التي
برعمت.

٣٨ يثبت ذكرياته
بدبابيس رصاصية
على حيطان
غرفته،
يجففها.
الصور
الورود
القبل
ورائحة الحب.
جميعها تنظر إليه

of bay leaves and honey
on our lips…

Because between us
there is no longer…

35   I apologize…
Unaware,
and unintentionally,
my breezes
shook your branches
and dropped
the only flower
you'd ever bloomed.

38   He fixes his memories
with small lead pins
on the walls
of his room
to dry them.
Pictures
flowers
kisses
and the scent of love.
They all look at him

بعين الامتنان الحانية
لأنه جعلها
خالدة.
تقريباً خالدة!

٣٩ من وقت لوقت
يفتح الشبابيك
ومن وقت لآخر
يغلقها.
ظله يفضحه
من وراء ستائره
يذهب ويعود
يقترب ويبتعد.
يرفع صوت الحاكي
يعبئ بالموسيقى وحدته
موهماً الجيرة
بأن كل شيء كالمعتاد.
كنا نراه
يمر بسرعة،
مطرق الرأس
حاملاً خبزه؛
وعائداً
إلى حيث
لا أحد ينتظره.

with eyes full of tender gratitude
because he made them
eternal,
almost eternal.

39   From time to time
he opens the windows,
and every now and then
he closes them.
His silhouette betrays him
behind his curtains
as he comes and goes,
his travels, far and near.
He turns up the radio
to fill his solitude with music,
deceiving the neighbors
that all is well.
We used to see him
hurrying past,
his head downcast,
carrying his bread
and returning
to where
no one waited for him.

٤٠   ما كان يريدُ
اكثرَ من ذلك،
بيتاً
وأطفالاً وزوجة
تحبـه.
إلا أنه استيقظ يوماً
ليجدَ رُوحَه
قد هرمت.

ما كانت تريدُ
أكثر من ذلك،
بيتاً وأطفالاً
وزوجا يحبها.
استيقظت يوماً
لتجـد
أن رُوحها
قد فتحت نافذة
وانطلقـت.

٤٢   هذا المساء
سيخرجُ رجل،
يبحث عن
فريسة
تُشبِع سِرَّ شهواته.

40   He wanted
no more than this:
a house,
children and a wife
who loved him.
But he woke up one day
and found that his spirit
had grown old.

She wanted
no more than this:
a house, children
and a husband who loved her.
She woke up
one day
and found
that her spirit
had opened a window
and fled.

42   This evening
a man will go out
to look for
prey
to satisfy the secrets of his desires.

هذا المساء
ستخرج امرأة
تبحث عن
رجل يجعل منها
سيدةَ سريره.

هذا المساء
ستجتمع الفريسة والصياد،
سيختلطان،
وربما..
ربمـا
سيتبادلان الأدوار.

٤٤   لم يكن يخجل منها
بملابسه القطنية القديمة
وجواربه المثقوبة.
أمامهـا
كان يتعرى كما
تتعرى
حاجاتُ الحب،
ليهبط
كالمَلَك
على جسدها.

This evening
a woman will go out
to look for
a man who will make her
mistress of his bed.

This evening
predator and prey will meet
and mix
and perhaps
perhaps
they will exchange roles.

44   He felt no shame before her
in his old cotton clothes
and his torn socks.
He undressed,
the way the need for love
strips naked,
and descended
like an angel
upon her body.

٤٥ لديه امرأتان،
واحدة تنام في سريره
وواحدة تنام في سرير حلمه.

لديه امرأتان تحبانه،
واحدة تشيخ قربه
وواحدة تمنحه صباها
وتأفل.

لديه امرأتان
واحدة في قلب بيته
وواحدة في بيت قلبه.

٤٦ مســاءً
خذها من خصرها،
قبّل عُنُقَها كما قبلتني،
وامسح بيديك
تعبَ نهارها المُضني.
قل لها ــ من أجلي ــ
مازالت جميلة
وشهية
كيوم عرفتها.
ضاجعها كما تحب أن تضاجعَني
حتى تغرّد
طيورها الساكنة،

45   He has two women:
     one sleeps in his bed,
     the other sleeps
     in the bed of his dreams.

     He has two women who love him:
     one ages beside him,
     the other offers him her youth
     then droops.

     He has two women:
     one in the heart of his house,
     one in the house of his heart.

46   At night
     take her by the waist.
     Kiss her throat as you kiss me
     and wipe with your hands
     the fatigue of her exhausting day.
     Tell her—for me—
     that she is as beautiful
     and desirable
     as on the day you met her.
     Make love to her
     the way you make love to me,
     until her silent birds
     begin to chirp—

المرأة
التي هي...
غريمتي!؟

٤٧ أتت كلها،
برائحة سريرها
ومطبخها،
بقبلات زوجها
المخبأة تحت قميصها،
بسائله
الذي لا يزال ساخناً
في بطنها.

أتت،
بتاريخها وأحلامها،
بتجاعيدها
وابتسامتها المقشبة،
بالزغب الذي يعشعش
على حافة وجنتيها،
بأسنانها
التي علق عليها بقايا فطورها.

أتت بكل آلامي
المرأة التي يعيش معها رجلي.

the woman
who is
my adversary!

47 She came whole,
  with the smell of her bed
  and her kitchen,
  with her husband's kisses
  hidden under her blouse,
  with his liquid
  still hot
  in her belly.

  She came
  with her history and her dreams,
  with her wrinkles
    and her reedy smile
  and the fuzz adorning
  the edges of her cheeks,
  with her teeth
    and the remains of her breakfast
    between them.

  She arrived with all my pains
  the woman my man lives with.

٤٨ هي التي
استباحت
رجلَ امرأة أخرى
فأدخلته سرها
ومنحته شهوة جديدة
وجسداً.

هي الشريرة
التي يسمونها
آكلة الرجال
صادقة
أعطته قلبها
ليأكله.

٤٩ في شهقة اللحظة
التقينا.
عبرتني،
وعبرتك.
منحتني ألمي،
ومنحتك فخرك.
ستذهب لتروي
أرضا جديدة،
وسأبقى أنا واجمة:
كيف
تشابكت أيدينا.

48   She is the one
     who seized
     another woman's man,
     and let him into her secret
     and gave him a new pleasure
     and a body.

     She is the evil one
     they call
     a man-eater
     who innocently
     gave him her heart
     to devour.

49   In the heaving of a moment
     we met.
     You crossed me
     and I traversed you.
     You gave me my pain
     and I gave you your pride.
     You will go to water
     a new earth,
     and I will remain ponderous:
     How did
     our hands get entangled?

٥١   على الفراش
بقعة حمراء
مبللة بدموع شهوة عذراء.
تُحِب لأوَّل مرة
وتَغْتسل بماء الحياة الأبدي.
ذلك العرق
الساخن
وروائحه الغريبة
التي تنبثق
من جسدين
يحتفلان
بموت الرغبة.

٥٢   جاءني
متخفياً في جسد رجل
فلم آبَهْ به.
قال لي
افتحي
فأنا الروح القدس.
وخوفاً من المعصية
تركته يقبلني،
عرّى
بنظراته
نهديّ الخجولين؛
حوّلني لامرأة جميلة.
ثم نفخ في جسدي روحه
هـادراً

51   On the bed,
     a red spot
     wet with the tears of a virgin desire.
     She loves for the first time
     and bathes in the eternal water of life —
     that hot
     sweat
     and its strange scents
     emanating
     from two bodies
     celebrating
     the death of desire.

52   He came to me
     disguised in the body of a man
     and I ignored him.
     He said:
     Open up!
     I am the holy spirit.
     I feared disobeying him
     so I let him kiss me.
     He uncovered
     my shy breasts
     with his gaze
     and turned me into
     a beautiful woman.
     Then he blew his spirit into my body,

رعداً و صواعقَ.
آمنت.

53 علمها أن
تتفتح
كزهرة رمّان حمراء،
أن تُنصت
لوشوشَات جسدها،
وأن تصرخ،
بدل أن
تَئِد آهاتَها،
وهي
تسقط
كورقة مرتعشة.

57 كان عليك
ألا تمسك بيديّ،
لتترك لهما
الحلم بلمسك.

كان عليك
ألا تقبّل شفتيّ،
لتجعلهما
تحترقان للثمك.

rumbling thunder and lightning.
And I believed.

53   He taught her
     to open up
     like a pomegranate blossom,
     and to listen
     to the whispers of her body,
     and to scream out
     instead
     of muffling her sighs
     as she
     fell
     like a trembling leaf.

57   You should not
     have touched my hand
     and left it dreaming
     of your touch.

     You should not
     have kissed my lips
     and left them burning
     for your muffling caress.

كان عليك
أن تصمت،
كي لا أتوقف عن
الأمل.

٥٩ كنت أسير على السراط
المستقيم
عندما اعترضت طريقي
اختل توازني
إلا أنني
لم أقع.

٦٠ بفاكهتي الجميلة
أضيء
الطريق المؤدي إلي.

طيورك الغبية
تحب
الخبز اليابس.

٦٢ سأغمض عينيَّ،
ولن أقوم بحراسة
معبدك.

You should have
remained quiet
so that I would not stop
hoping.

59   I was on the straight
     path
     when you blocked my way.
     I stumbled
     but I did not
     fall.

60   With my delicious fruit
     I light
     the way leading to me.

     Your stupid birds
     prefer
     old bread.

62   I will close my eyes,
     I will not guard
     your temple.

هذه المرة
سأدع
الإله العربيد
يهرب حافياً.

٦٣ باركني حرة
واصبر
على تمنعي.
اقترب عندما
أدعوك،
وعندما
أهملك،
تعلم انتظاري.
أقبلني لغيرك
وتعلم الحب.

٦٤ كانت تأتيه
لتهبه
مساماتها
وأناملها
المزينة بالكَرَز
يأكلها بنهم.

This time
I will let
the mischievous god
escape barefoot.

63   Bless me with freedom
and be patient
with my refusal.
Come closer when
I invite you,
and when I neglect you,
learn to wait.
Desire me for someone
other than yourself
and learn to love.

64   She set out
to offer him
her pores
and her nails
adorned with cherries,
which he ate
ravenously.

كانت تذهب
وسَلَّةُ قلبها
فارغــــة.

٦٥   يتكُّور صدري
بشوق الرغبة،
رغيفاً ساخناً
تقضمه
أسنانُ
عبثِك.

٦٦   لن آتي
إلى حيث ينتظرني،
في المكان القريب الذي أعرفه.

ها أنا أغسل شعري
فيما إذا أراد أن يداعبَه،
وأضع الرائحة التي يحب
فيما إذا اقترب ليَضُمَّني.

لن آتي
إلى حيث ينتظرني،
سأربط قدمَيَّ
وستنتابني الحمَّى.

She left
with the basket
of her heart
emptied out.

65   My chest swells
with a longing for lust,
a hot loaf of bread
bitten
by the teeth
of your folly.

66   I will not go
to the place where he waits for me,
the nearby place I know well.

Here I am washing my hair,
in case he wants to caress it,
and putting on the perfume he loves
in case he comes close to embrace me.

I will not go
to the place where he waits.
I will bind my feet,
and a fever will strike me.

ها أنا ألبس معطفي و أخرج:
خروفٌ صغير
ذاهب للمذبح.

٦٨   كل مساءات أيامه
كان يخطط
رحيلها
فيتألم.

كل صباحات أيامه
كان يدخلها حجره
فيسعد برؤيتها
تدفئه بحبها.

كان ينتظر المناسبة
ليقول لها ارحلي،
وفي كل مناسبة
لا يجد المناسبة.
جائعة وهو الوليمة
عارية وهو ثيابها.

ينساها
فهي لا تأخذ مكاناً،
وعندما يتذكرها
يجدها تحت إبطه؛
يقتلها
فيرى قدمها

Here I am putting on my coat and leaving:
a lamb
heading for slaughter.

68   Every night
he planned
her departure
and it pained him.

Every morning
he placed her in his hovel,
and it pleased him to see her
warm him with her love.

He waited for the right time
to tell her to leave.
But every time
he could not find the time.
She was starving and he was her feast;
she was naked and he was her clothes.

When he forgot her
she seemed to disappear,
and when he remembered her
he found her nosing his armpit.
He killed her
then saw her feet

في حذائه
وبطنها الحار
على جسده.

كان يجد نفسه
جميلاً في سريرها
وهي تبعثر برفق
حاجبيه المرتبين،
وتمسح بشعرها
غبار صدره.

قضى عمره
يفكر
كيف لرجل مثله
أن يترك
امرأة
مثلها.

٦٩ لم تنفع
فساتيني
التي اشتريتها جديدة،
ولا النظرات
الدافئة
التي كنت أرمقه بها.
لم تنفع كلمات الحب،
ولا نصائح أوفيد.
لا شعري الأسود الطويل

in his shoes,
and her hot belly
resting against his side.

He found himself
beautiful in her bed
as she softly disheveled
his well-groomed eyebrows,
and as she swept with her hair
the dust off his chest.

He spent his life
thinking
how a man like him
could leave
a woman
like her.

69 The new dresses
I bought
did not help,
nor the warm
looks
I tossed him.
My tender words did not help,
nor Ovid's counsel.
Not even my long black hair

ولا طراوة جلدي اللامع.
لم تنفع لهفتي
ولا عذوبتي
لا ابتساماتي ولا دموعي
أن تطوّع
قلب الحب
القاسي.

٧٠   عصفورٌ
يموت في يدي،
لم يعد
دافئاً وطريّاً
لا هواجس
تسكنه
ولا أحلام،
يموت كيومٍ بلا حب.

٧١   حضنت
جذعك.
هززته
ألماً،
فانهمرت
قطرات نداك
على جرحي.

or my glowing soft skin.
My lust did not help,
nor my sweetness,
nor my smiles and tears,
to soften
the hard heart
of love.

70   A sparrow
          dies in my hands.
It is no longer
          warm and soft.
No thoughts
occupy it now,
       and no dreams.
It dies like a day without love.

71   I embraced
your trunk,
I shook it
with pain,
and drops of your dew
fell into
my wound.

٧٢ لن يكون
أَلَمُكَ
اكثر من وخزة إبرة
وأنا أدير ظهري.
سيكون ألمي
أحمرَ
كَمَصْرِ كرزة ناضجةٍ
على بلاطٍ
أبيض،
وأنا أراقب
ابتسامةَ الخلاص
عَلى طَرفِ فمك.

٧٣ الأفعى ستموت
عندما
تلســعني
و تـذوق
ألـمي.

٧٤ تجلوها
كشمس لعيني سجين
تبسطها
كزُهور البنفسـج
تحت حذاء عسكري.
تمنحها

72 Your pain
    will not be
    more than a pinprick
    as I turn to leave.
    My pain
    will be red
    like a ripe cherry mashed
    on a white
    tile
    when I see a smile
    of relief
    on the side of your mouth.

73 The serpent will die
    when
    it bites me
    and tastes
    my pain.

74 You reveal it
    like the sun to a prisoner's eyes.
    You spread it
    like narcissus flowers
    under soldiers' boots.
    You offer it

كريمة كَثَدْي أمٍ
تفتتها كالخبز
لطيور جائعة...

ماذا ينفع
أن تعري الروحَ هكذا
أمام
من لا يرى.

٧٥   حب آخر يموت؛
 سترتبه المرأة بخنوع
في خزانة ذكرياتها
المليئة
بطيور أحلامها
المحنطة.

٧٧   لملم بيديك
باقة
خصري الطرية
من على السرير
المليء بأشلاء
الضحايا...

64

generously like a mother's breast.
You crumble it like bread
for hungry birds…

What good does it do
to undress the soul this way
before one
who cannot see?

75   Another love dies:
     Submissively the woman
     will place it
     in the wardrobe of her memories
     filled
     with the embalmed birds
     of her dreams.

77   Gather in your hands
     the bouquet
     of my soft waist
     from a bed
     full of the victims'
     severed limbs.

٨٠ ماذا فعلت بغيابك؟
غَيَّرت ماء حوض السمكة الحمراء،
سقيت النبتة الصغيرة،
رتّبت أنفاسي،
و بدأت أنسجُ
كنزة الصوف!

٨٢ كالكتب المحرّمة
أخفيك تحت وسادتي.
تنامُ الأضواء
تنامُ الأصوات
فأخرجُك
وأبدأ
بالتهامِك.

٨٣ لا تنظر إلى هذه الكدمة
الزرقاء،
ولا إلى الجرح
الذي يعلو قلبي.
لا تنظر
إلى التجاعيد التي بدأت تحفر
حول عيني،
ولا إلى الشعرات البيضاء
التي تنبت في رأسي.

80 What did I do in your absence?
    I changed the water
    in the goldfish bowl,
    I watered the small plant,
    I regulated my breathing
    and began knitting
    the woolen sweater.

82 I hide you under my pillow
    like a forbidden book.
    The lights sleep
    and the sounds sleep.
    Then I take you out
    and begin
    devouring you.

83 Don't look at the blue
    bruise
    or the wound
    above my heart.
    Don't look
    at the wrinkles that began to scratch
    the edges of my eyes,
    or at the white hairs
    sprouting from my head.

فقط
لرُوحي..
روحي
عشبُ آذار الجديد.

٨٥ سلطان النوم
المستبد
يسرقك مني.

وحيدة قربك،
أعد النجوم المعلقة على أهدابك
وأجس
نبض وقتي المحتضر
في فمي بقايا كلمات
وفي أصابعي رغبة
لا تستكين..

٨٧ عندما تخرج
من حذائك
وتتركه
وحيداً
على عتبة الباب
أو تحت السرير

Look only
to my soul,
my soul
the new grass of March.

85 Sleep,
that merciless tyrant,
snatches you from me.

Alone beside you
I count the stars suspended from
your eyelashes
and take the pulse
of my dying time —
word scraps in my mouth,
and in my fingers
an unstoppable urge.

87 When you take off
your shoes
and leave them
lonely
on the doorstep
or under the bed

يحتله الضجر
وأقدام الانتظار الباردة.

٩٠   معلقة
كذرات الهواء
على معطفك.
كنقطة ماء على حافة
ذقنك.
كعنكبوت بين الفراغ
والفراغ.

كمصير
بين شفتي الله.

٩١   مللت البقاء
على هامشك
في مسوداتك
على أدراجك
أمام أبوابك.
أين
فسيح جنانك؟!

they are filled by boredom
and the cold feet of waiting.

90   Suspended
     like air particles
     on your coat,
     like a drop of water
     on the tip
     of your chin.
     Like a spider between emptiness
                         and emptiness.
     Like a destiny
     between God's lips.

91   I am bored with being
     in your margins,
     in your notebooks,
     in your traces,
     before your doors.
     Where
     are the wide spans of your heavens?

٩٢   تعال عارياً
     لأُلبسك
     جسدك
     الذي استعاره خيالي.

٩٣   نظرت إلى مرآتي
     فرأيت
     امرأة
     مليئة بالرضى
     ذات عيون مضيئة
     وخبث لذيذ

     حسدتها.

٩٥   قولوا للريح
     أن تهدأ
     فأنا لا أُحب الريح
     إنها قادرة
     كامرأة غيور
     على أن تنبش شعري
     وأنا ذاهبة
     لأقابل
     الذي ينتظرني.

92   Come naked
      that I may dress you again
      with your body,
      which my imagination
      has borrowed.

93   I looked into my mirror
      and saw
      a woman
      filled with contentment.
      She had bright eyes
      that looked with delicious mischief,

                             and I envied her.

95   Tell the wind
      to calm,
      for I don't love the wind.
      It can
      like a jealous woman
      mess up my hair
      as I go out
      to meet
      the one who waits for me.

قولوا للمطر
أن يتوقف
فأنا لا أحب
المطر.
إنه قادر
كزوج غيور
على أن يبلل ثيابي
وحذائي الجديد،
وأنا أنتظر
ذلك الذي
لم يأت.

٩٦   لحسن الحظ
لديّ قلم
وورقة
يخففان
وطأة انتظارك،
و إن لم...
سآكل أظافري
وأركل بعصبية
النمل
الذي بدأ يتسلق ساقي.

Tell the rain
to stop,
for I don't love
the rain.
It can
like a jealous husband
drench my clothes
and my new shoes
as I wait
for the one
who has yet
to arrive.

96   Fortunately
I have pen and paper

                to lighten
                the pain of waiting for you.
                If not…

I would gnaw at my fingers
and nervously kick
at the ants
that have begun to climb
my trunk.

٩٧ أعطني كذباتك
أغسلها
أُدخلها براءة قلبي
أجعلها حقائق.

٩٨ تختلف عنهم كثيراً...
علامتك الفرقة
قبلتي
على فمك.

١٠٠ لم يكن ذَنْبك
لم يكن ذنبي.
هي الريح
أوْقَعت
مشمشةَ شهوتي
الناضجة.

١٠٢ أنا وفرحي
ننتظر
رفيفَ خطواتِك.

97   Give me your lies.
I will wash them
and tuck them into
the innocence of my heart
to make them facts.

98   You are very different from them...
Your distinction:
My kiss
is on
your mouth.

100   It was not your fault.
It was not my fault.
It was the wind
that brought down
the ripe apricot
of my desire.

102   My happiness and I
await
the flutter of your steps.

١٠٣   كحبات ملحٍ
كانوا يلمعون
ثم ذابوا.
هكذا رحلوا
هؤلاء الرجال
الذين لم يحبوني.

١٠٥   أنا في البرد
والعتمة،
لماذا
لا تفتح لي
بابَ قميصِك.

103   Like grains of salt
        they shone
        then melted.
        This is how they disappeared,
        those men
        who did not love me.

105   I am out in the cold,
        in the dark.
        Why
        don't you open the door
        of your shirt to me?

من

أنـظـر إلـيـك

٢٠٠٠

from

I Look to You

2000

١ لنا وجوهٌ
نحملُها على أكتافِنا
على بطاقات هوياتِنا
في صُوَرِنا التذكارية

لنا وجوهٌ
نمزِّقُها نحفظُها
نخبِّئُها نكشفُها
نألفُها نُنْكِرُها
نحبُّها
و نكرهُها

لنا وجوهٌ
نعرفُها...
نقولُ: نعرفُها؟

٢ "هنالكَ
دائماً من يشبهُنا
في مكانٍ ما"
قالتِ العاهرةُ الصغيرةُ
و هي تبتسمُ بثقةٍ
ناظرةً الى النافذةِ
و كأنَّها تَرى
حُلْمَها
شجرةً موفورةَ
الثمـار..

82

1   We have faces
we carry on our shoulders,
on our identity cards
and family pictures.

We have faces
we shred and keep,
hide and reveal,
faces we become accustomed to
and shun,
that we love
and hate.

We have faces
we recognize...
And we say: Recognize?

2   "There's always
someone who resembles us
somewhere in the world,"
said the little prostitute
smiling with assurance,
looking at the window
as if she saw
her dream
shaped like a tree
laden with fruit.

٣ الرمّانةُ
المحتَفِظةُ بأسرارِ
لآلئها
لا تزالُ تنتَظِرُ
أن تخلعَ
قِشرتَها اللامعة..

العطشُ موعودٌ
بسائلٍ
طيِّبْ..

٤ أستطيعُ أن أميّزَها
مِنْ بينِ كلِّ
القبلاتِ
تلكَ التي تطبُعُها الرغْبَة.

أستطيعُ أنْ أعرِفَها
مِنْ كلِّ
الرغباتِ
تلكَ
التي يؤجِّجُها
الحُبّ..

3   The pomegranate
guarding the secrets
of her pearls
still waits
for her shiny skin
to be disrobed.

Thirst is promised
a sweet
liquid.

4   I can tell it apart
from all
the kisses
desire has stamped on me.

I can recognize it
among all
the desires
that
love
emblazons.

أيُّ
جُرمٍ جميلٍ
اقترفتُ؟

تمتَّعتُ
بجسَدٍ
أهداني
نهراً مُسكراً
و إنتفاضةَ حياةٍ..

ماذا بوسعِها أنْ تفعلَ
أمامَ موجةٍ عارمةٍ كهذِهِ
في حرٍّ كهذا؟

زَبَدُ البحرِ
لامسَ بطنَ قَدَمِها
فانتابَها
شعورٌ من القشعريرةِ
أنساها
الصلاةَ..

ماذا أسمعُ؟
تفتُّحَ وردةٍ
و صهيلَ جَوَادٍ..

5   What
    beautiful crime
    have I committed?

    I enjoyed
    a body
    that gave me
    a soporific river
    and an upheaval of life.

6   What could she have done
    in a heat wave like this
    on a hot day like this one?

    Sea foam
    touched the arch of her foot
    and she was swallowed
    by a wave of trembling
    that made her forget
    her prayers.

7   What do I hear?
    A rose opening
    and a horse neighing...

ماذا أرى؟
سُحباً
تتوهَّجُ في حُضْني
و مَطَراً
يَهْطُل..

٨ قالت: نَعَمْ
التهِمْتُهُ..
كنتُ جائعةً
كَرَجُلٍ..

و كَرَجُلٍ
طَرَحَتْهُ رغْبَتي
مُزْدَهِرةً بذكورَتِها..

٩ أعْدُو أركضُ أتمهَّلُ أصعَدُ
            أهبِطُ
أدنو أبتعِدُ
        أصرخُ
أئِنُّ ألْهَثُ أصْمُتُ أضيعُ
أتواجدُ
        أعصِفُ أُمطِرُ
        أبكي أضْحَكُ..

What do I see?
Clouds
gleaming in my lap
and rain
pouring...

8   She said: Yes
I devoured him...
I was hungry
like a man...

And like a man
I splayed him across my desires
blossoming with masculinity.

9   I run   jog   I tarry   rise

                    and descend
I come close   move away

                    I scream
I moan   pant   fall quiet

                    disappear   and become
I storm   I rain
I weep   I laugh

امرأةٌ في عُرسِ شهوَتِها
تضِجُّ بملائكةِ رَجُلٍ..

١٠ كفقيرٍ يأكُل
حتّى التُّخمةِ
خوفاً من يومٍ
لا طعامَ فيهِ

أنظرُ اليكَ
في حُضْني..

١١ أفتِّشُ عَنْ قِطَعِ
ثيابي
لتَلْبَسَني.

أُلمِلمُ بصمْتٍ
دموعَ
اللَّذة..

أتخلَّصُ من براهينَ مُروري
تاركةً ايّاكَ
غائباً عن الوعي لرحيلي
قتيلاً طريًّا
كأنَّكَ نائمٌ..

A woman in the feast of her ecstasy
thronged by a man's host of angels.

10   Like a tramp
overstuffing himself
dreading a day
without food

I look to you
in my lap.

11   I search for pieces
of my clothes
to wear me.

I gather in silence
tears
of pleasure.

I erase all evidence of my arrival
leaving you
unconscious of my departure.
A tender corpse
as if you were asleep.

١٣   نَسْمةَ هواءٍ
أَنسلُ بينَ
شَفَتَيْ بابِكَ
مثلَ نَفَسٍ أخيرٍ
ولا تَتَشبَّثُ بي..

١٤   لا تكُنْ فاتراً
فأتقيَّؤُكَ..

اشتَعِلْ
مِثْلَ
جَمرةٍ
مِثْلَ
احتكاكِ غُصنَينِ
تَوهَّجْ..

هكذا أُحبُّ
الحياةَ
في مَضْجَعي.

13   A breeze,
      I slip in
      between the lips of your door
      like a last breath
      and you do not cling to me.

14   Don't be so stale
      that I have to vomit you.

      Spark up
      like
      an ember.
      Like
      the rubbing of two branches
      flame up!

      That's how I love
      life
      in my bower.

١٥   سَتَسْكُنُكَ
رائِحتي..
و عندما تَتعرَّى
ستعْبَقُ
مُتَّهِمةً إيّاكَ
بخيانتي.

١٦   كلُّ ما أملِكُ
أفرُشُهُ
كَعُشْبٍ..

أصابِعُكَ تُحرِّرُني
طليقةً أُصبِحُ
كريحٍ..

١٧   الرَّغَباتُ
عواصِفُ
تَرتَطِمُ بحاجزٍ
(ممنوع المرور)

طريقُكَ
لا يَمُرُّ في شارعي..

94

15   My scent will
       invade you,
       and when you undress
       it will spread and spread
       accusing you
       of betraying me.

16   All that I own
       I spread around me
       like grass.

       Your fingers release me,
       and free I become
       like a gust of wind.

17   Desires are
       storms
       that crash against a barrier
       (NOT A THROUGH STREET).

       Your path
       does not run along my street.

١٩   قالتْ سينامُ العنكبوتُ
     بينَ خيطانِهِ
     مصائرُ الفراشاتِ
     الضالّة..

     سيتغذّى
     بجَهلِها..

٢٠   أعرِفُ أنَّهُ
     لم يكُنْ عَلَيَّ
     أنْ أدعَهُ
     يكشِفُ عن نَهديَّ
     كنتُ أُريدُ
     فَقَط
     أنْ أريَهُ
     أنَّي امرأة..

     أعرفُ أنَّهُ
     لم يكُنْ عَلَيَّ
     أنْ أتركَهُ يتعرّى
     كانَ
     يُريدُ
     أن يريَني أنَّهُ
     رجُلٌ
     فَقَط..

19   She said the spider will sleep—
in his web
will be
the destinies of wayward moths.

He will feed
on their ignorance.

20   I know
I shouldn't have
let him
uncover my breasts.
I only
wanted
to show him
I'm a woman.

I know
I shouldn't
have let him
undress.
He only
wanted
to show me
he's
a man.

٢١   بكثيرٍ مِنَ الحنانِ
إكشِفْ أغطيتَها
برفْقٍ
ضَعْ أصابعَكَ
على جَسَدِها.

إمرأةٌ سهلةٌ؟
ربَّما
إمرأةٌ مهجورةٌ؟
حتماً..

٢٢   ... وكَشَفَ لي
عُرْيَهُ
جوعَ جَسَدِهِ
وجوعَ روحِهِ
و ما تركَ العُمْرُ
مِنْ بُثورٍ
و جُروحٍ
مِنْ جَمالٍ و قُبحٍ...

غَطَّيتُهُ
بلِحافِ الرَغْبَة..

21 With great affection,
    lift her covers,
    and with tenderness
    place your fingers
    on her body.

    An easy woman?
    Perhaps…
    An abandoned woman?
    Certainly…

22 …and he showed
    his nakedness,
    the hunger of his body,
    and the hunger of his soul
    and what time had imprinted
    in scabs
    and wounds,
    in beauty and ugliness.

    I wrapped him
    in the blanket of desire.

٢٣   قالتْ: لنتصنَّع الحُبَّ
في شِبهِ سريرٍ
يَضمُّ
شِبهَ رَجُلٍ
شِبهَ امرأةٍ

بعواطفَ
شِبهِ حقيقيةٍ
فارشينَ حَولَنا
وروداً شِبهَ ميّتةٍ
لكيْ لا تموتْ..

٢٤   جلـدُكَ
يجِفُّ
ينضُبُ
ينشَـفُ
يـقحَـلُ
يتَشَـقَّقُ ..
جِلـدُكَ
يُؤلِمُكَ..

عَرَقي لم يَهطُلْ عليه..

23   She said,
      "Let's pretend to make love
      in a pretend-bed
      that includes
      a pretend-man
      a pretend-woman

      with emotions
      that are almost real
      spreading around us
      almost-dead flowers
      so that they would not die."

24   Your skin
      dries
      itches
      flakes
      blisters
      cracks up.
      Your skin
      hurts you.

      My sweat has not poured upon it.

٢٧   أقيسُ مدى استطاعتي
خيانَتكَ
بأنْ أتخيَّلَكَ
في حُضْنِ امرأةٍ أُخرى..

فأتوبُ
و أستغفرُكُ..

٢٨   أرجوكَ
أن تأتيَ..

لقدْ طلبتُ فنجانَ القهوةِ
وخوفاً أنْ
أتأخَّرَ
نسيتُ
مِحفظةَ نقودي..

٢٩   يسيلُ عليها لعابُ الآلهةِ
وَهيَ
تَنْتَظِرْ..

27   I measure my ability
to betray you
by imagining you
in another woman's embrace.

Then I repent
and seek your mercy.

28   I beg you…
come…

I've ordered a cup of coffee
and fearing that
I'd be late
I forgot
my purse.

29   The gods' mouths
drool
on her
as she
waits.

لا بُدَّ
أنَّكَ نسيتَ
أوراقَكَ
فَعُدتَ على أعقابِكَ..

أو أنَّ
صديقاً اتَّصلَ
ثمَّ راحَ يُثرثرُ
و أنتَ تهمُّ بالخروجْ..

أو لا بُدَّ
أنَّكَ تنتظرُني
في مقهىً آخَرْ..

حَسِبتُها ٣٢
خطواتِكَ
دقّاتُ
قلبيَ
المتلاحِقَة..

قالتْ: رُبَّما ٣٣
ما زالَ الحُبُّ
يَنْتَظِرُ..

30 You must have
    forgotten
    your papers
    and returned to retrieve them.

    Or
    a friend must have called
    and begun to chatter
    as you were about to leave.

    Or you must
    be waiting for me
    in another café.

32 I thought
    they were your steps
    those quick
    tremors
    in my heart.

33 She said, "Perhaps
    love is still
    waiting."

مِظلَّةٌ تَحْتَ كُرسيٍّ
كتابٌ على مِقعدٍ
امرأةٌ تَحْسَبُ أنَّهُ
سيأتي..

٣٥   لا...
ليسَ بابُكَ
الذي أُطرُقُ
و الذي
أَسمعُ
خَلْفَهُ
أنفاساً
و الذي
رَغْمَ انكسارِ مِصراعَيْهِ
لا يَفْتَحُ..

٣٦   يَعرِفُ
رائحةَ إِبْطي
مسامَّ جِلدي
طَعْمَ لُعابي..

رَجُلٌ مَنحَني ماءَهُ
و منحْتُهُ مائي..

106

An umbrella under a chair,
a book on another.
A woman who thinks love will
come.

35   No...
It's not your door
I'm knocking on.
It's not the one
behind which
I hear
breathing.
It's not the one
broken off its hinges,
which still refuses
to open.

36   He knows
the scent of my armpits,
the pores of my skin,
the taste of my saliva.

A man who gave me
his water
and whom I gave
my water.

رَجُلٌ خانَ
ذاكرتَهُ..

٣٧   ستهجُرُني؟
إذنْ
مَنْ سيرى
فُستانَ عُرِي
الذي أبدو فيهِ
حَقّاً
جميلة؟

٣٩   سيقتَفي أثَرَكَ
خَيَالي
إن ذهبتَ
خطوةً خطوةً
أمامَكَ
خطوةً خطوةً
خلفَكَ..

كالذَّئْبِ
أشدُّني اليكَ
ولا أريدُ الخَلاص..

A man who betrayed
his own memory.

37   You'll abandon me?
     Who will
     then see
     the attire of my nakedness
     in which I appear
     truly
     beautiful?

39   My shadow
     will follow your traces
     step by step
     as you go
     forward,
     and step by step
     as you go
     back.

     Like sin
     I cling to you
     never desiring salvation.

٤٠   أمامَ صَدرِكَ
أربُضُ
أُلملِمُ
زَفيرَكَ
أخبِّئُهُ ليومِ اختناقي..

٤٣   رَجُلٌ لَهُ فَمٌ
و لا يتكلَّمُ
شَفَتانِ
و لا يُقَبِّلْ..

رَجُلٌ لَـهُ أَنْفٌ
و لا يَشُـمُّ
له أذنانِ و لا يَسْمَعْ..
رَجُلٌ له
عينانِ حزينتانِ
و ذراعانِ طويلتانِ
لا تعرفانِ العِناقْ..

رَجُلُ القَشِّ
خَدَعَ
عصافيري..

40   By your chest
     I crouch
     and gather
     your exhales
     for the day of my asphyxiation.

43   A man who has a mouth
     but does not speak,
     has lips
     but does not kiss.

     A man who has a nose
     but does not smell,
     has ears but does not hear.
     A man who has
     sad eyes
     and long arms
     that do not know
     how to embrace.

     A scarecrow
     has tricked
     my sparrows.

٤٤ سيُثقِلُ ضِلعَهُ
هبوبُ أنفاسِها..

سيضيقُ سريرُهُ
الحائطُ أمامَهُ
و هيَ خلفَهُ..

ستتذمَّرُ قدماهُ
فلمْ يَعُدْ لهما فُسْحَة..

قليلاً و ترحَل
سيتمطّى بطولِ ذراعيهِ
و سيفلشُ صُرَّة أضلاعِهِ
مُدركاً حينَها
أنَّ الحائطَ ما بَرِحَ أمامَهُ
و خلفَهُ
هاويـةُ
فراغِها..

٤٥ ليسَ من السُكَّرِ
و العَسَلِ..

مصنوعٌ مِنَ التَعَبِ
و الهمومِ
مِنَ الذكرياتِ
و الأحلامِ

44 His ribs will be burdened
    by her breathing.

    His bed will grow small—
    the wall before him
    and her body behind him.

    His feet will grumble—
    nowhere for them to go.

    A little while and she'll be gone.
    He will stretch the length of his arms' span.
    He will empty out the bundle of his ribs
    and then realize
    the wall is no longer before him,
    and behind him
    there is the abyss
    of her absence.

45 Not of sugar
    or honey...

    He's made of fatigue,
                              worries,
    memories
                              and dreams,

مِنَ القسوةِ
و الجَفافِ
مِنَ العُشـبِ و الماءِ
مجبولٌ بالوهمِ
و الخوفْ..

٤٦   قلبٌ مثقوبٌ
برصاصاتِ الخيبةِ المُتَتالِيَة..

٥٢   إنه يَئِنُّ
يتوجَّعُ
أَيِّلٌ يَحْتَضِرْ..

كمْ رصاصةً بقيَ؟
وَكَمْ
من رحْمَـة..

٥٣   ماذا يفعلُ جَوادٌ
بعُنُقٍ جميلٍ
مكسورْ؟

hardship

              and drought,
of grass and water,
wound up in illusions
and terrors.

46   A heart punctured
by consecutive bullets of failure.

52   He is moaning
in pain,
a deer breathing his last.

How many bullets are left?
How much
mercy?

53   What does a horse do
with a beautiful broken
neck?

٥٤ كان مُخْتَفياً
عندما فجأةً
عادَ و احتلَّ غُرفةَ الجلوسْ..

صَعَدَ من القبو
تمدَّدَ على الأريكةِ
غَيَّرَ محطّةَ التِلِفزيون
غَيَّرَ محطّةَ الراديو
ثُمَّ...
ثُمَّ راحَ يتمشَّى بسروالِهِ الداخليِّ
كأنَّهُ في بيتِهِ

تعرَّى..
ولم تكُن تَرى
سوى
رَجُلٍ نَسِيَتْهُ..

٥٦ ثيابٌ قديمةٌ
تملأُ خِزانَتَها
و أطفالٌ يأتونَ
مساءً
بضجيجٍ
و نتائجَ ضَعيفَة..

116

54   He was hiding,
then suddenly
he returned and took over the living room.

He climbed from the basement
and stretched out on the sofa.
He changed the TV channel,
changed the radio station,
then
began to pace in his underwear
as if he were in his own house.

He undressed
and she saw nothing
except
a man she'd forgotten.

56   Old clothes
fill her wardrobe,
and children
come
in the evening
with a loud din
and low test scores.

زوجٌ هَجَرَها
و عشيقٌ لم يعُدْ لَدَيهِ
وقتْ..

٥٧ في الشارعِ المؤدّي
إلى منزلِها
صالونُها مضيءٌ
طيفُها
يتأرجَحُ
كقنديـلْ..
تريدُ من اللهِ
أنْ يلوّحَ لها بمِروَحةِ
نسائِمِه
أو يُبَلْسِمَ بأنفاسِهِ
حُروفَها
كأُمٍّ حَنونْ..

٥٩ الصمتُ يحضُنُ
المنزلَ المُعْتِمَ
كعشيقٍ جديدْ..

المرأةُ في السريرِ الكبيرِ
تنتَظِرُ
شِبهَ يائسةٍ
مجيءَ النُعاسِ

A husband who abandoned her,
and a lover who no longer has
the time.

57 On the street
to her house
her living room appears lit
and her silhouette
swings
like a lantern...
She wants God
to wave at her
with the fan of his breezes
or to balm her burns
with his breath
like a kind mother.

59 Silence enfolds
the dark house
like a new lover.

The woman in the large bed
waits
almost desperate
for the coming of sleep,

الذي هَجَرَها
أيضاً...

٦٢ قالتْ: بقيَ
جدارٌ
بِبَصَمَاتٍ سوداءَ
و ظِلالٍ
ينتظرُ عِنايَتي..

وحدَها الجدرانُ
لا تُبارِحُ
بلْ تزدادُ
التِصَاقاً بي..

٦٣ نسيتَ
أنَّها أُنثى

تلكَ التي نظرتَ
إلى حُزنِها
كفُقاعاتِ صابونٍ
و تَلَهَّيْتَ بأظافِرِكَ
وَهْيَ
تَغْرَقْ..

which too
has abandoned her.

62   She said: There remains
a wall
with black fingerprints
and shadows
that needs my care…

Only walls
stay put.
Rather they seem to be leaning
toward me.

63   She forgot
she was a female,

she who looked
at her sadness
as if it were bubbles,
and distracted herself
with your fingernails
as she
drowned.

٦٥   البيتُ مُتعَبٌ
غُرَفُهُ العُليا
لم تَعُدْ مأهولةً..
البيتُ يُعاني الصمتْ..

في الجهةِ الشماليَّةِ
شَقٌّ
تأتي منهُ العواصفُ
و خيوطُ الماءِ المُخْضَرَّة..

مشلولٌ
لا يستطيعُ الركضَ
و لا الذهابَ الى حيثُ يُحِبُّ

كَمْ كانَ يحلُمُ بسعاداتٍ بسيطةٍ
كَمْ توخّى الجَمَالَ
و كَمْ حَزِنَ لرؤيةِ جُدرانه تتقشَّر
و صُفرةُ الدخَّانِ و الزَمَنِ
تعتلي بَياضَه..

٦٨   نافذةٌ
نِصْفُ مفتوحةٍ
نِصْفُ مُغلَقةٍ
نافذةٌ
نِصْفُ مغطَّاةٍ
نِصْفُ مكشوفةٍ
نافذةٌ

122

65   The house is tired,
its upper rooms
no longer lived in.
The house throbs with silence.

In the north corner
a crack
where storms blow in
and threads of green water flow.

Crippled
it can't run
or go where it wishes.

How it dreamt of small happinesses,
how it aspired to beauty,
how sad it was to see its walls peel
and the yellowness of smoke and time
crawl up its whiteness!

68   A window
half open
half closed.
A window
half covered
half uncovered.
A window

نِصفُ مُضيئةٍ
نِصفُ مُعْتِمةٍ
تُطِلُّ على حائطٍ
تُطِلُّ على حديقةٍ
على شارعٍ
على عُشْبٍ
على إسـفلتٍ
عـلى أسـوَدَ
عـلى أخْـضَرْ..

نافذةُ الحُبِّ..

٦٩   خَيَالانِ
لو تمعّنتَ جيّداً
لمَيَّزْتَ ذِراعينِ
ثُمَّ نَهدينِ..

امرأةٌ مُنهَمِكةٌ حتَّى الغياب
في حُضْنِها رأسُهُ
تعجِنُهُ تُكَتِّلُهُ، تُدَوِّرُهُ، تَلُفُّهُ..
يداهُ تُعَرِّشانِ على جِذْعِها..

تدورُ حولَهُ
يدورُ حولَهَا
تركعُ أمامَهُ
يركعُ أمامَهَا

124

half lit
half dark
facing a wall
facing a garden
a street
grass
asphalt
facing black
facing green.

The window of love.

69   Two apparitions—
     if you looked closer
     you'd notice two arms
     and two breasts.

     A woman, busy and absentminded.
     His head is on her chest.
     She kneads it, molds it,
     she turns it, and wraps it
     while his hands rest on her trunk.

     She swivels around him.
     He swivels around her.
     She bends before him.
     He bends before her.

تَغسِلُهُ
و يَغسِلُها
تُهيِّئُـهُ
يُهيِّئُها..

في حَمَّامِ البيتِ المقابِلْ..

٧٠   البعُوضةُ
و ليستْ عودةُ زوجِها
ما أيقظَ
آلامَها
بعدَ مُنْتَصفِ الليل..

عَرَفَتْ هذا
من البصَماتِ الحمراءِ
الملتهبةِ
التي وَجَدَتْها
على خَدِّها..

٧١   لماذا نَسيتَ
أن تُطفىءَ
قبلَ أن تنامَ
مِصباحَ
رَغْبتي المتوهِّجَ؟

She washes him
and he washes her.
She prepares him
and he prepares her.

In the bathroom
of the house opposite...

70   A mosquito,
     not her husband's return,
     is what awakened
     her pains
     after midnight...

     She became aware of this
     from the red fingerprints
     she found
     flaring
     on her cheek...

71   Before you fell asleep
     why did you forget
     to switch off
     the lamp
     of my burning desires?

تَركُتَني
مُضيئةً
لطيورٍ شَرِسَة..

٧٣   قالت: لِماذا لا يأتونَ
محمَّلينَ بسعادتِهمْ
و نَجاحِ أطفالِهمْ
ذكرياتِهمْ
و مشاريعِهمْ
يُشاركونَني
عَشائي ؟!

٧٤   بيتُ أصدقائي
قريبٌ
و بيتي
بعيـــدٌ   بعيــــدْ..

٧٥   ورَّثَتْ أطفالَها
أُمّاً تَحْلُمُ
تَرقُصُ
تبتَسِمُ

You left me,
a bright and radiant target
for birds of prey.

73   She said, "Why don't they come
bearing their happiness
and the successes of their children,
their memories,
their plans,
and share a meal
with me?"

74   My friends' houses
are close,
and my house,
far, far away.

75   She bequeathed her children
a mother who dreams,
dances,
and smiles.

أمَّاً تبكي
تَعْشَقُ

أمَّاً لا تَمْلِكُ مالاً
ولا ترفو جَوارِبَ

أمَّاً تكتُبُ أشعاراً
بِلُغةٍ لا يفهَمونَها..

٧٦   خاسِرةٌ
       كمُهْرةٍ
       امْتَطاها فارسٌ
       خائِبُ..

٧٧   زَقْزَقاتُ العصافير
       خُضْرةُ الحديقةِ
       التي تُزْهِرُ
       أمامَ عينها
       الهدوءُ
       والأيَّامُ
       التي كانتْ تَمضي
       دونَ أن تَرقُصَ
       دونَ أن تُغَنِّي
       دونَ أن يَطْرُقَ بابَها زائرٌ

A mother who weeps
and loves.

A mother without money
and who doesn't mend socks.

A mother who writes poems
in a language they don't understand.

76 She lost out
    like a mare
    ridden by
    a doddering horseman.

77 The sparrows' song,
    the greenness of the garden
    flowering
    before her eyes,
    the quiet,
    and the days
    that passed
    without her dancing,
    without her singing,
    without a visitor knocking at her door,

أو أنْ يرنَّ هاتفُها
ما قَتَلها..

٧٨   لم تكُنْ تُفكِّرُ بشيءٍ
أو
هذا ما كانَ يبدو
لم يكُنْ هناكَ مَطَرٌ
ولا عواصفُ شديدةٌ...

لم يكُنْ هناكَ
داعٍ
أوُ
هذا ما كانَ يبدو
كى تُمسكَ سِكِّيناً
وتقطعَ
شِريانَ ثوبِها..

٨٠   ثَمَّةَ عيونٌ
لا ترى الضـوءَ
ثَمَّةَ ذكرياتٌ
لا تُذْكَرُ..

ثَمَّةَ ابتساماتٌ لا تَمْنَحُ الفَرَحَ
ثَمَّةَ دموعٌ لا تَغْسِلُ الألَمَ
ثَمَّةَ كلماتٌ تَصفَعُ

without her phone ever ringing,
is what killed her.

78   She wasn't thinking of anything
    or
    that's how it seems.
    There was no rain pouring down
    or severe storms.

    There was no
    reason,
    or
    that's how it seems,
    for her to take a knife
    and sever
    the arteries of her dress.

80   There are eyes
    that see no light,
    there are memories
    never remembered.

    There are smiles that give no joy,
    there are tears that wash away no pain.
    There are words that slap,

ثَمَّةَ مشاعرٌ
ثَمَّةَ روحٌ
لا عَزَاءَ لها..

٨٢ بخُطى الهِرِّ
الرشيقةِ
بِصَمْتِها
اخْتُطفني وهُمْ نِيامٌ..

لا تنسَ أنْ ترسُمَ
ابتسامةً على وجهي
لتهدِّىءَ
رَوعَ أطفالي
صباحاً
عندما يُقلِقُهُم
غِيابي...

٨٦ تزَحفُ ببطءٍ
لكُن
بثقةٍ
أشْعُرُ بها تدنو

أُنصِتُ
إنَّها تلهَثُ
كَمَن يحاولُ

there are feelings,
there is a soul
that cannot be consoled.

82   With a cat's nimble
silent
steps,
kidnap me as they sleep.

Don't forget to draw
a smile on my face
to calm
the children
in the morning
when my absence
frightens them.

86   She crawls slowly,
but
with confidence.
I feel her coming closer.

I listen.
She is panting
like someone

تَسلُّقَ حائطٍ
أَملَسْ..

٨٩   مباركٌ بطنُكِ
الملِيءُ
بالرغباتِ و الخوفِ..
صدرُكِ العارمُ الذابلُ..
فمُكِ الذي
يَسيلُ صوتاً
و مياهاً..
أصابعُكِ
التي تكتُبُ
التي تَمْسَحُ
التي تبني
التي تَهدِمُ..
مُبَاركةٌ
شهواتُكِ
و آلامُكِ..
مُبـاركٌ
عَبَثُكِ..

٩٠   ألَم يكونوا
مشـرَّدينَ
فآويتِ
جِياعاً

136

trying to climb
a slippery wall.

89   Blessed is your belly
filled
with wishes and fears,
your robust, crumbled, wilting chest,
your mouth that
drips with sound
and water,
your fingers
that write
that erase
that build
that destroy.
Blessed
your desires
and pains.
Blessed
your futility.

90   Were they not
destitute
and you housed
the hungry

فأطعمتِ
خائفينَ
فأسبلتِ على قلوبِهِمْ
الطمأنينة
و أنتِ تَعْلمينَ
أنَّهُمْ
كالعواصِفِ
عابرونْ..

٩٢   يُثْقِلُونَ
أكتافَ يومِها
بكثيرٍ
من قليلٍ
حُبِّهِمْ..

٩٤   كلُّهُمْ لها
كلُّهُمْ
لها..

الذينَ
تُحِبُّهم و يُحبُّونَها
تُحِبُّهم و لا يُحبُّونَها..

تأخذُهُم
من أحضانِ أسرَّتِهم

and fed
the terrified
and spread comfort
about their hearts
knowing
they were
like storms
always passing…

92   They burden
the shoulders of her day
with a great deal
of their meager
love.

94   They're all hers.
All of them
are hers…

Those
she loves and who love her,
she loves and who don't love her.

She takes them
from the embraces of their beds,

من مشاغِلِهِمْ و هُمومِهِمْ
تغسِلُهُمْ
تُعطِّرُهُمْ
تُجمِّلُهُمْ
يكفي..
أن تُغمِضَ عَيْنَيْها
و تَحلُمْ..

٩٥   دعِهِمْ يُقْبِلُونَ
فوقَ جِمالِهِمْ
مؤمنينَ بالرؤيةِ
يهتَدُونَ بنَجْمَةٍ..

الأبوابُ الموصَدَةُ
ستُفتَحُ
عندما يَسْجِدونَ
بتواضُعِ الملوكِ
ليقدِّموا عندَ
سريرَكِ
صلواتِهِمْ..

٩٧   كم تُرِكْتَ
لتُصبِحَ فَزِعاً..

140

from their concerns and worries.
She washes them,
perfumes them,
beautifies them.
It suffices her
to close her eyes
and dream.

95   Let them come,
riding their camels,
believing the vision,
guided by the star.

The shuttered doors
will open.
And they will prostrate
with the humility
of kings
to offer,
by your bedside,
their prayers.

97   How long have you been
abandoned
to be startled so…

كم تألَّمْتَ
لتُصبحَ قاسياً..

وكَمْ بينَ هذا
وذاكَ
تُفاجِئُني بِكَ
يا حُبّ..

٩٨   سأمحُو
عَنِّي آثارَ الليلِ
بقُطْنٍ
وحليبٍ
وماءِ وَرْدُ..

سأخلَعُ دِفْأَهُ
كثوبِ نَوْمي
أرميهِ
على أقربِ كُرسيٍّ
لأستقبلَ
النهارَ
عشيقيَ المُضيء..

How long have you suffered
to have become so cruel...

And how often between this
and that
have you surprised me
O love...

98   I will wipe
the traces of the night
off of me
with cotton
and milk
and rose water,

I will strip his warmth
like a nightgown
and toss it
on the nearest chair,
to greet
daylight,
my luminous lover.

٩٩   كُلَّما غادَرَني
رَجُلٌ
أزدادُ جَمالاً.

١٠٠   أزدادُ..

99   Whenever a man
     leaves me
     my beauty increases.

100   Increases...

About the Author

Maram al-Massri is a Syrian poet and translator living in France. Originally from Latakia, she studied English Literature at Damascus University, and started publishing in the 1980s. She has published three books of poetry and won the Adonis Prize for Poetry in 1997 and the Premio Calopezzati in 2007. Her work has appeared in many international anthologies and been translated into French, English, Spanish, Corsican, Serbian, and Italian.

About the Translator

Khaled Mattawa is the author of three books of poems, *Ismailia Eclipse, Zodiac of Echoes,* and *Amorisco* (forthcoming). He has translated five volumes of contemporary Arabic poetry and co-edited two anthologies of Arab American literature. Mattawa has received a Guggenheim Fellowship, a National Endowment for the Arts translation grant, the Alfred Hodder Fellowship from Princeton University, and three Pushcart Prizes. He teaches in the M.F.A. Creative Writing Program at the University of Michigan, Ann Arbor.

Copper Canyon Press gratefully acknowledges
Lannan Foundation for supporting the publication and
distribution of exceptional literary works.

LANNAN LITERARY SELECTIONS 2007

Maram al-Massri, *A Red Cherry on a White-tiled Floor: Selected Poems*

Norman Dubie, *The Insomniac Liar of Topo*

Rebecca Seiferle, *Wild Tongue*

Christian Wiman, *Ambition and Survival: Becoming a Poet*

C.D. Wright, *One Big Self: An Investigation*

LANNAN LITERARY SELECTIONS 2000–2006

Marvin Bell, *Rampant*

Hayden Carruth, *Doctor Jazz*

Cyrus Cassells, *More Than Peace and Cypresses*

Madeline DeFrees, *Spectral Waves*

Norman Dubie, *The Mercy Seat: Collected & New Poems, 1967–2001*

Sascha Feinstein, *Misterioso*

James Galvin, *X: Poems*

Jim Harrison, *The Shape of the Journey: New and Collected Poems*

Hồ Xuân Hương, *Spring Essence: The Poetry of Hồ Xuân Hương,*
  translated by John Balaban

June Jordan, *Directed by Desire: The Collected Poems of June Jordan*

Maxine Kumin, *Always Beginning: Essays on a Life in Poetry*

Ben Lerner, *The Lichtenberg Figures*

Antonio Machado, *Border of a Dream: Selected Poems,*
  translated by Willis Barnstone

W.S. Merwin
  The First Four Books of Poems
  Migration: New & Selected Poems
  Present Company

The Chinese character for poetry is made up of two parts: "word" and "temple." It also serves as pressmark for Copper Canyon Press.

Since 1972, Copper Canyon Press has fostered the work of emerging, established, and world-renowned poets for an expanding audience. The Press thrives with the generous patronage of readers, writers, booksellers, librarians, teachers, students, and funders—everyone who shares the belief that poetry is vital to language and living.

Major funding has been provided by:

Anonymous (2)
Beroz Ferrell & The Point, LLC
Lannan Foundation
National Endowment for the Arts
Cynthia Lovelace Sears and Frank Buxton
Washington State Arts Commission

Copper Canyon Press gratefully acknowledges the following individuals for their generous Annual Fund support:

Linda Breneman
Rhoady and Jeanne Marie Lee
Brice Marden
Jan North
Charles and Barbara Wright

For information and catalogs:

COPPER CANYON PRESS
Post Office Box 271
Port Townsend, Washington 98368
360-385-4925 · www.coppercanyonpress.org

English text set in Galliard, designed for digital composition by Matthew Carter after the sixteenth-century designs of Robert Granjon. Arabic text set in Sakkal Majalla, designed by Mamoun Sakkal after simplified Naskhi fonts. Book design and composition by Valerie Brewster and Mamoun Sakkal. Printed on archival-quality paper at McNaughton and Gunn.